SECURE
YOUR CHILD'S
FUTURE

11 Smart Ways to Invest for Enough Cash
Flows at Right Time

SECURE YOUR CHILD'S FUTURE

11 Smart Ways to Invest for Enough Cash
Flows at Right Time

By

SAMEER KAILA

Worldwide Published by
Pendown Press

PENDOWN PRESS

An ISO 9001 & ISO 14001 Certified Co.,

Regd. Office: 2525/193, 1st Floor, Onkar Nagar-A,

Tri Nagar, Delhi-110035

Ph.: 09350849407, 09312235086

E-mail: info@pendownpress.com

Branch Office: 1A/2A, 20, Hari Sadan, Ansari Road,

Daryaganj, New Delhi-110002

Ph.: 011-45794768

Website: PendownPress.com

First Edition: 2020

ISBN: 978-93-90479-85-6

Layout and Cover Designed by Pendown Graphics Team

Printed and Bound in India by Thomson Press India Ltd.

WHAT THE CLIENTS SAY ABOUT AUTHOR

Mr. Sumit, who was handling financial on his own, met me and this is what he has to say:

> *"Sameer is helping me create fund for higher studies of my children. He has also guided me to protect my family with appropriate Life and Health covers."*

Mr. Sen, a senior person in a corporate, was investing all his savings in fixed deposits and paying 30% tax on his interest income, has to say this:

> *"Sameer has not only helped me in my investments that suits my risk profile and enabled me getting better returns, but also helped me in saving 30% tax on FD interest that I was paying year on year. I was reluctant in taking health insurance. He logically explained me and got me and my family covered with Health Cover. Thanks Sameer."*

CONTENTS

INTRODUCTION

Hello, My Name is Sameer Kaila. I am a Financial Expert and a business owner of firm Dhancreators.

My tryst with capital markets began more than 21 years ago. It has been a long journey; I have seen lots of highs and lows in capital markets. I have come across numerous cases wherein people have invested without having financial objectives and requisite cash flows in mind, and have struggled thereafter. To make my experience count for the benefit of families (either salaried or entrepreneurs), bankers, retirees, parents looking for investments for children, in 2016, DhanCreators was established with an objective to create roadmap and help them achieve Financial Milestones. The journey has been extraordinary, wherein I have been able to establish and nurture longlasting relationships with the clients.

As you already know the longterm investments are the main vehicles to realize our big dreams for our safe retirement as well as for fulfilling our big dreams for our children's higher education and marriages. But alas! Many people commit financial blunders and their investment planning fails, leading to financial turmoil in their lives, especially at the time of dire need.

In a quest to guide our clients to protect their dreams, I have created this book with the sole objective that investors would read this book before they start their investment journey, and will be able to stick to roadmap of achieving their financial milestones.

I have kept it simple and have added few questions for you to ask to yourself, so as to help you identify whether there is any gap between your aspirations, planning and execution; and bridge the gap, if any.

I am confident that this booklet will be beneficial for you and your family and will add value in your financial know how.

Happy Investing !!!

CHAPTER 1

FAILING TO PLAN IS PLANNING TO FAIL

Suresh, 45 has been working with an MNC firm and has salary of Rs. 2 Lakh per month. He lives with his wife, (who is a homemaker,) and 2 kids aged 15 and 12 respectively.

Suresh had been working in the firm for almost 12 years since now and has progressed from managerial level to senior position in the firm. I met him last year at a family function and discussed about Goal Planning. After a brief discussion, we decided to meet next Sunday at his place to discuss his objectives in detail. In the meantime, I gathered some more information about Suresh. He stays in his parental home and has a car loan with an EMI of Rs. 15,000/- per month, with 2 years of EMI left. Both Kids are school going with a monthly fee of Rs. 20,000/- per month. Neither he, nor his wife calculates the household expenses.

"It's not how much money you make, but how much money you keep, how hard it works for you, and how many generations you keep it for."

–Robert Kiyosaki

I went to his place and found that the family was facing basic financial challenges despite having decent income. I asked him what he has done for child education and his retirement. He replied almost instantly, "Sameer I haven't thought of any of the milestones as yet". His answer was We will cross the bridge when we come to it (see how to go about it at that time only).

Thereafter, I tried to structure it in such a way that eventually helped Suresh understand the Importance of Planning and Investing.

Friends, this is not the only case. I have seen families struggling to achieve their financial milestones such as creating funds for educating their children, planning for retirement years, etc. The main reason is, they don't plan in advance, and once the milestones are in front of them, either they borrow or have to be dependent on others for the accomplishment of their goals.

Most investors blindly invest in instruments that appear to be performing well. They usually get stuck in those investments and repent thereafter. The downside of not having a proper plan in place is that, you have no end goal, and as a result, the investment pattern becomes quite erratic. This, in turn, could turn you into a reckless investor, resulting in greater losses if you're not careful.

The simplest way to keep yourself from making this investment mistake is to take some time to chart out a financial plan before you begin investing. Identify your goals and pick a strategy. Keep a track of your investments and take corrective actions, if required, and stay invested till the objectives are met.

> *"Do not save what is left after spending; instead spend what is left after saving."*
>
> **–Warren Buffett**

I asked Suresh and his wife to write down their Financial Goals and asked them to note down present cost. They were in a state of shock when they saw that education inflation @ 10% per annum and lifestyle inflation @ 6% per annum will double the expenses in 7 and 12 years respectively. I also made them calculate, the amount they need to invest per month to reach the desired outcome. They realised the mistake of not investing at early age, which could have resulted in lower outflow of funds and given power of compounding to the investments.

I shared following rule which I also follow – If you save and invest 30% of your income for financial goals, you won't have monetary problem in life, and all your milestones will be achieved.

Ask yourself

What are my Financial Goals?

____

____

____

____

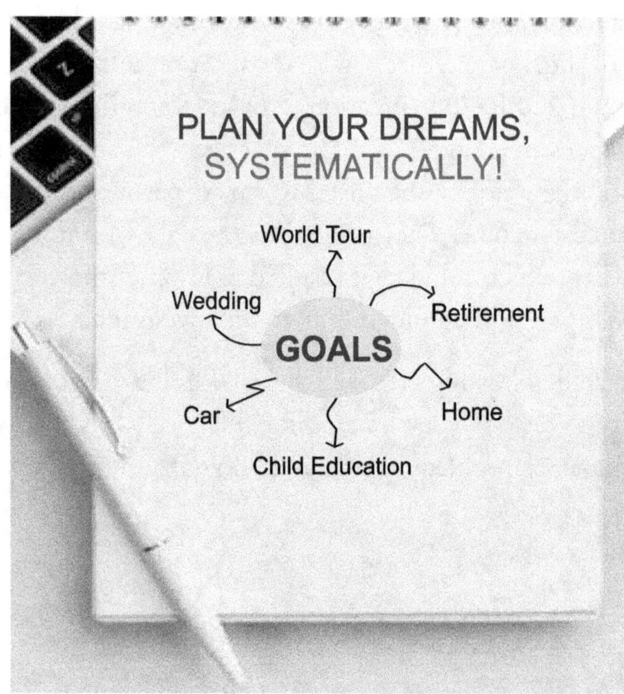

IMPULSIVE SPENDING IS INJURIOUS TO WEALTH

While discussing with Suresh, the first and foremost reason that came to light was, Suresh and his wife were impulsive spenders. They never created a budget and moreover did online shopping via portals, went to Shopping Mall without a fix amount to spend or a list and came back buying unnecessary items, overspending on discount schemes. I helped them realize it is one of the reasons they are not able to save and plan for their goals.

Don't medicate stress and fatigue with impulse buying. A shopping spree will set you back even more.

—Rochelle Greene

Impulsive spending is common problem in households nowadays. With nuclear family structure and easy access to internet and funds and all the e- commerce websites pushing Sales, people tend to purchase goods which are not necessary and later repent on those purchases.

Impulsive buying is the tendency of a customer to buy goods and services without planning in advance. When a customer takes such buying decisions at the spur of the moment, it is usually triggered by emotions and feelings.

I asked Suresh and his spouse to take following steps to control Impulsive spending :

- Plan your purchases

- Create a budget

- Differentiate between Needs and Wants

- Give yourself time to think

- Beware of SALE Traps, especially ONLINE

- Don't give yourself access to easy money.. Credit cards, etc.

Ask Yourself

Instances where you did Impulsive buying for which you later regretted. What action will you take to control it?

____

____

____

CHAPTER 3

START EARLY-
MAXIMIZE POWER
OF COMPOUNDING

During further discussion with Suresh, I came to know that in the name of savings and investments, he has 7 lakh of investments in fixed deposits @ 7% per annum and is having a recurring deposit of Rs.10,000/- per month without any financial objective. I asked him about his EPF amount he said, he changed his job a year back and withdrew his EPF and family went to Europe with the money, so he doesn't have enough in EPF account. Here, Suresh did a big mistake by withdrawing his EPF savings which could have compounded till his job. He neither invested in Equity Markets nor in Mutual Funds in his life, since he is of the view that people incur losses in equity markets. It was a firefighting task to create a corpus for the elder child's higher studies. Suggested him to start a SIP in Debt Fund/ increase recurring deposit to accumulate.

> *"Investing puts money to work. The only reason to save money is to invest it."*
>
> *–Grant Cardone*

Most of the investors start investing once they reach in their mid 30s or early 40s and could miss the power of compounding, since they have less time to avail the power of compounding to create a decent corpus in equity markets.

One should start investing as and when he or she starts earning. All the financial longterm milestones need sufficient time for reaping the astonishing results of the 'Power of Compounding'. Staying invested for 15/20/25 years can give 3-4X returns to the investments as a result of power of compounding.

Do it Yourself: What is your equity exposure?

Hint: 100 – your age = Investment in Equities

Here is a suggestible investment and target amount one can calculate to achieve the Rs. 25 Lakh amount for higher studies. In the above case, Suresh needs to invest approximately 1 lakh per month (64173 and 35511) for both children to reach the desired amount.

Age of Child when you start investing	Monthly Investment Required	Investing Horizon	Target Amount @ 8%
3 Years	INR 7,672	15 years	2500000
6 years	INR 10,778	12 years	2500000
8 years	INR 14,380	10 years	2500000
10 years	INR 23,348	8 years	2500000
12 years	INR 35,511	6 years	2500000
15 years	INR 64,173	3 years	2500000

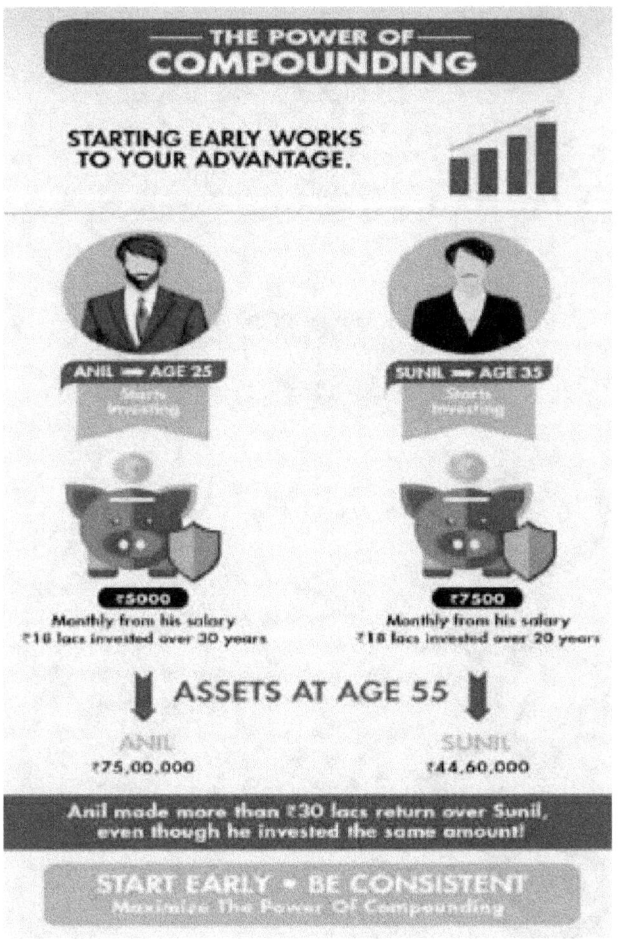

The Returns have been calculated @ 8% CAGR.

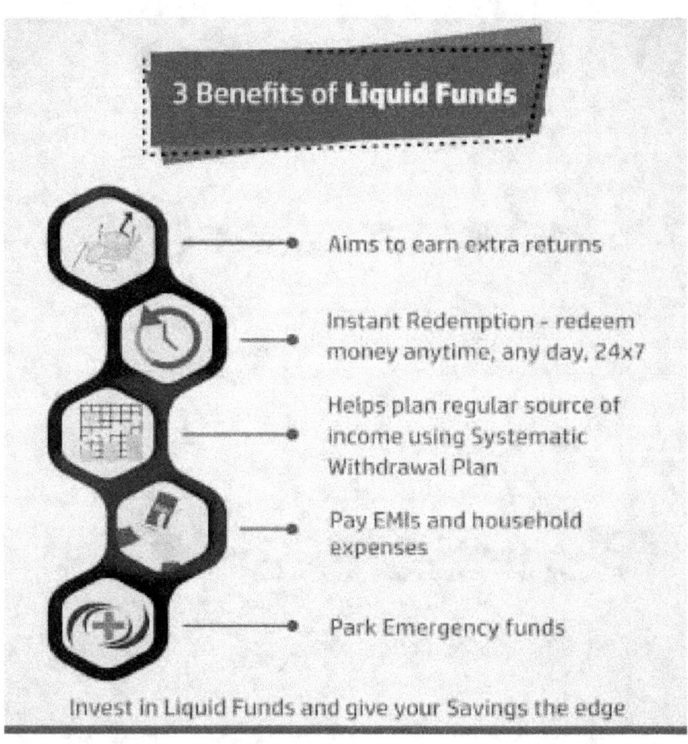

3 Benefits of Liquid Funds
Aims to earn extra returns
Instant Redemption - redeem money anytime, any day, 24x7
Helps plan regular source of income using Systematic Withdrawal Plan
Pay EMIs and household expenses
Park Emergency funds
Invest in Liquid Funds and give your Savings the edge

CHAPTER 4

CREATE EMERGENCY FUND

We took the discussion ahead and came to know that Suresh has 7 Lakh FD and approximately 5 Lakh of amount in his Savings account, which could take care of approximately 6 months of his monthly income, which is sufficient in normal times. But, that's the only savings that he has.

Your emergency fund is not an investment,
it's insurance with one purpose—to
protect you and your family.

—Anonymous

People tend to ignore the importance of having enough emergency fund in place, and this can land them in serious trouble such as job loss, salary cuts, business recession, medical emergencies etc. Not having adequate emergency fund leads them to borrow at high rates or break investments meant for long-term goals.

Solution

- One should create at least 1 year of emergency fund
- To Take care of expenses (Household & Business) for that period of time.
- Liquid fund SIPs/Recurring deposit/ Fixed Deposits are best medium

Ask Yourself

How much Emergency Fund have you created?

____

____

Insure your Family with "ADEQUATE"
LIFE & HEALTH Covers.

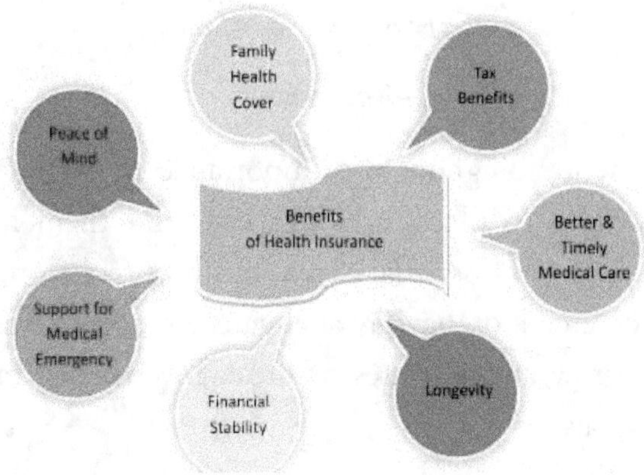

CHAPTER 5

ADEQUATE LIFE/ HEALTH INSURANCE COVERAGE

HEALTH COVERAGE

Once I discussed about investments, I moved to protection part with Suresh since I feel, it is the backbone of a family. I asked him about Health Coverage. Since I had heard this answer from most of the working professionals, I got the same answer, "I have got Corporate cover of 5 Lakhs." I again asked him, "Do you have Personal Family Floater Cover?"His answer was "I don't need that, why should I spend amount over there since I have coverage from my office?" I put across him the following questions:

You need health insurance till the time you need (good) health.

—Dinesh Verma

(1) Are you married to your company?

(2) Is your company going to employ you life long?

(3) Are you never going to retire?

(4) What will happen to your child education, in case you use that fund for hospital bills?

(5) What happens if your company coverage gets exhausted?

(6) What happens if due to any lifestyle disease in future, insurer refuses to give you and your family, the health cover or there is very high loading?

Suresh realised that his savings could go for a toss in case there is some medical emergency and he immediately took a decision of opting for a Family Floater Health Cover of 10 Lakhs.

Medical Expenses tend to gradually increase as a person grows old. Most people say, I have corporate cover of 5 Lakhs for my family, Do I need a personal cover as well? India's healthcare inflation has been rising steadily and more alarmingly, it is increasing at double the rate of overall retail inflation.

The No. 1 cause of bankruptcies is medical bills

–Michael Moore

With the ever-increasing medical costs, @15% per annum, it becomes vital to ensure that you have enough health cover or health corpus that can take care of various unexpected medical expenses from time-to-time. It needs to be enhanced after every 5 years to take care of inflation component. As there is Credit history in Credit Card, there is Health history with the Insurer. Early you start, a better health score you will create with the insurer.

Ask Yourself

How much Health Cover do you have for yourself and family and from which Insurer ?

____

____

____

____

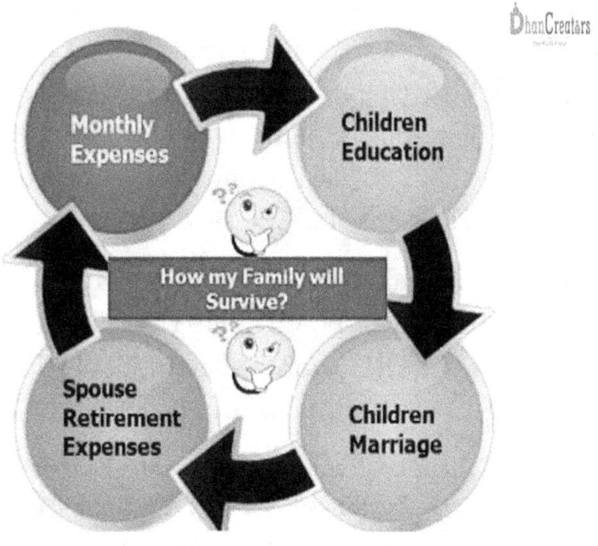

LIFE COVER

Biggest RISK in LIFE is LIFE itself. If the earning member is not around the family anymore, what about daytoday expenses, child education milestones of the family?

Staying on protection with Suresh, I asked him about his life covers. He proudly went inside his house and brought a file which had 5 LIC policies wherein he was paying Rs. 1 Lakh per annum for 15 to 20 years as premium and will get back approximately 40 Lakhs, and his coverage was not even 20 lakhs. I asked his wife "Bhabhiji, what is his value for you and your family"? She replied "He is invaluable to the family, without him we won't be able to survive and our children won't be able to accomplish higher studies as per their dreams." Suresh was sitting numb. I gave him thumb rule of Life Insurance, to take life cover of 10-12 times of his annual CTC, i.e. approximately additional cover of 2 cr. Suresh immediately agreed to my advice and bought a Life cover of 2 Cr.

How one can transfer the risk? One should compulsorily buy a TERM INSURANCE PLAN to meet his life insurance needs. It helps to cover the RISK for the family. Ideally, TERM Cover should be 10-12 times of Annual Income.

> *"I don't call it "Life Insurance," I call it*
> *"Love Insurance." We buy it because we*
> *want to leave a legacy for those we love."*
>
> *—Anonymous*

Ask Yourself

How much Life Insurance Cover do you have and from which Insurer? Is it sufficient to cover your loans and family financial goals?

Answer:

____

____

____

____

Asset Allocation & Diversification leads to

- RISK Divergence

- Reduction exposure in one asset class

- Reduces Volatility

- Safeguards against Market Cycles

CHAPTER 6

DIVERSIFY YOUR INVESTMENTS

Diversification is important because it helps you balance risky assets against more stable options. Most investors simply construct their portfolio by having all their investments in one asset class, either Equities/Real-estate/Gold/Fixed Deposits or Fixed Income which is a bad idea and is like sitting on a Time Bomb which can blast anytime.

> *"Rule No. 1: Never lose money. Rule No. 2: Never forget rule No.1"*
>
> *— Warren Buffett*

In the above case, Suresh was inclined towards Fixed income basket only. He hasn't got any exposure to other asset classes like Equities/Gold/Real- estate etc. I suggested him to start investing in Equities through Mutual Funds through SIPs for education of children (Systematic Investment Plans). He could also start investment in Gold SIP through investing in a Gold Index Fund to diversify the risk.

Diversification of portfolio is a key to success while investment planning. One has to diversify the portfolio into Financial Assets as Stocks/Debt/ International Equities and Physical assets such as property and 5-10% allocation in Gold to produce consistent returns over the time rather than investing in a single asset class.

Ask Yourself

What is your Current Asset Allocation? Have you diversified among all asset classes, or is it skewed towards one asset class?

____

____

____

____

CHAPTER 7

BEAT THE INFLATION- THE MONSTER

Believe it or not, Rs 10,000 in 1982 was worth just Rs 552 in 2018, all thanks to inflation. While you may earn compound interest on your savings, whatever compound interest gives, inflation takes away. To put it another way - inflation is effectively the reverse of compound interest; it's like decompound interest.

Inflation is like toothpaste. Once it is out, you can hardly get it back in again.

Consider a situation where you invest Rs 1 lakh in a deposit which earns you 8 per cent a year. At the same time, prices are also (by and large) rising at the rate of 8 per cent a year. In such a situation, your compounding returns will just keep pace with inflation.

What this example actually tells you is that over a long period of time, you need a form of investment that is inflation-adjusted. While a lot of investors think that equity is risky, it requires a little bit of thinking to see that inflation is riskier. And to match inflation, and to get real returns on top of that, you have to latch on to something that goes up with inflation.

Ask Yourself

Are your investments able to beat inflation?

____

____

____

____

CHAPTER 8

SHARE YOUR ASSETS/LIABILITY DETAILS WITH FAMILY MEMBERS

We Indians usually don't talk about money with our partners. We usually don't share the information about the financial documents as well as the investments or insurance with our partners. This puts the family of the deceased person in crises.

"A will can save one's family from being put into a quagmired pit of legal conundrum, in case of death (which may even be untimely)." –Henrietta Newton Martin

Letting your partner know about the financial documents and your investment will help him/her in case of an unforeseen event. Creating a Will is also a way to protect your assets from creating unwanted disputes within the family.

Ask Yourself

Have you created Master File/Document wherein you have summarized all your investments, insurances and loans? If yes, with which family member you have shared the information?

____

____

____

____

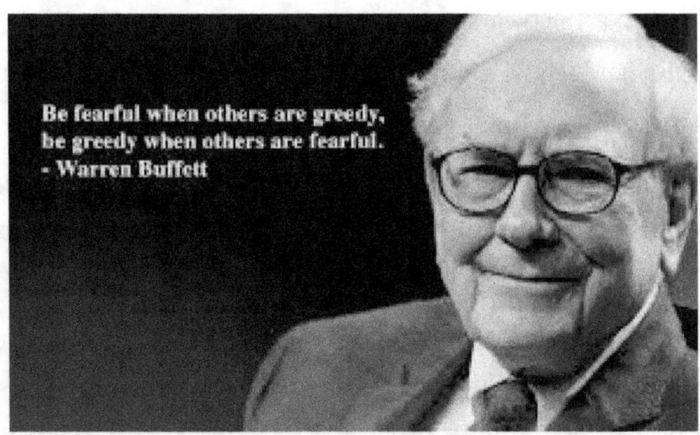

CHAPTER 9

DON'T EXIT FROM EQUITIES IN PANIC

Investors panic seeing equity investment portfolio drop 10% or more. When market falls, suddenly all factors become negative, all communication become negative and there is a sense of doom but things improve quickly as well.

Investors should not make the mistake that many did in 2009 or 2011 or in Oct., 2018 or March, 2020 by selling stocks from portfolio due to fear and then missing out on the recovery. Volatility is part and parcel of equity markets and panic selling must be taken as opportunity to invest rather than an opportunity to exit.

In above example, I categorically said to Suresh, "Equities is like Ocean, there are high tides and there are low tides, we have to ride both to reach the destination." I am very well aware that investor behaviour is very different when markets are up and his reactions are categorically different when markets are down, still those who have weathered the storm have created wealth, and that's the bottom line.

Ask Yourself

Have you ever exited Equity Markets in panic and later repented?

____

____

____

____

CHAPTER 10

CHECK YOUR RISK APPETITE
(BE HONEST TO YOURSELF)

(1) Please select the statement most applicable to you:

(a) I would rather protect my assets, even though there may be limited growth potential.

(b) I would rather experience steady growth each year.

(c) I would like high growth even though it may mean very volatile returns in the short term.

(2) Which of the following investment returns would most appeal to you if you were to invest an initial amount of Rs 2,00,000 for one year?

(a) A guaranteed amount of Rs. 210000

(b) Any amount between Rs. 200000 to Rs. 220000

(c) Any amount between Rs. 180000 to Rs 230000

(3) I am prepared to accept short-term losses if I believe the long-term returns will be good.

(a) Disagree

(b) Neutral

(c) Agree

(4) Which of the following statements best describes your investment philosophy?

(a) I feel comfortable with stable investments

(b) I am willing to withstand some fluctuations in my investment

(c) I am seeking substantial investment returns

Pl. check results and have you done investments in line with your risk appetite?

(A) Conservative Risk

(B) Moderate Risk

(C) High Risk

CHAPTER 11

TWO CHOICES

So, through this book, you are very well aware that one needs to plan his Financial Goals in advance before initiating investments. You also know that you need to refrain from impulsive spending and start investment journey from early age to maximize power of compounding, which is eighth wonder of the world.

Creation of emergency fund acts as a lifeline in times of crises. You should have 10-12 times of your CTC as Life Cover and must possess personal health cover for the family, which acts as a cushion in times of medical emergencies.

Now you also know that investing into one asset class is dangerous and you need to diversify your portfolio. Inflation is a big monster which is silently eating away our returns, and you must invest in those products which provide you positive net rate of return.

You are now aware that you must share your assets/liability details with family members. You must add equities in your portfolio when the markets are in panic and should not exit from them.

Above all, you must invest as per your risk appetite. Else you can suffer major losses if you invest without proper risk assessment.

Now, at this point in time, you have two choices.

One you go and identify all the road blocks that are there in Financial Investments and select suitable investment products on your own?? I have shared all the knowledge in this booklet that is worth knowing for you as an investor and hence you can move ahead and do your investments accordingly.

The second option is to **"Have Me By Your Side."** I will do complete analysis of your requirements, risk analysis, portfolio reviews from time-to-time and more importantly, will keep you on track till your financial milestones are met. Financial Investment journey is a long journey where lots of twists and turns will come and everyone needs a person for hand-holding at time of crises. I will stand by you to handhold you in those times.

You can get your Investment and Protection Audit done by me FREE of cost.

9 789390 479856